As Daniel London's concise introduction explains, *The Cloud of Unknowing* teaches us that God is not a thought or an idea, but a loving presence to be encountered in the simplicity of silence. Whether you have treasured this classic text for years or are coming to it for the first time, you will find something here that speaks to your soul and invites you more deeply into the life of prayer.

—Arthur Holder, PhD, Professor of Christian Spirituality, Graduate Theological Union, editor of *Christian Spirituality: The Classics* and *The Blackwell Companion to Christian Spirituality*

Like meeting an old friend after an absence and immediately being on intimate terms again, I met the essence of the beloved author of "the Cloud." This devotional brought me to tears and to belly laughs with that familiar wisdom and wink of slyness I have loved throughout my life. Daniel DeForest London has indeed distilled the author's authentic voice.

—Suzanne Guthrie, author of *Praying the Hours* and *Grace's Window: Entering the Seasons of Prayer*

To paraphrase a mystical work such as the 'Cloud' is no easy task but Daniel London managed to bring this classic jar down to the lower shelf, so to speak, and made it quite accessible to us all. Definitely a must read! Contemplative prayer suddenly has become for me a joy to engage in. Thanks to the author for crystallizing for us that love is the only instrument that can pierce through our own unknowing.

—Wil Hernandez, PhD, Obl. OSB, Executive Director of

CenterQuest and author of a trilogy on Henri Nouwen and *Accidental Monk: A Chronicle of Struggle, Faith, and Surrender*

As both a scholar and ordained minister in the Episcopal Church, Daniel London is able to do what few others are capable of today: a modern rendition of a "spiritual classic" that is both faithful to the original text, as well as immediately accessible and immensely rewarding to the contemporary reader. A fitting guide for either the classroom or personal spiritual sustenance, this edition is bound to become a "classic" in and of itself.

—David M. Odorisio, PhD, Director of the Retreat at Pacifica Graduate Institute, co-editor of *Depth Psychology and Mysticism* and editor of *Merton and Hinduism: The Yoga of the Heart*

THE CLOUD OF UNKNOWING, DISTILLED

REV. DR. DANIEL DEFOREST LONDON

APOCRYPHILE
PRESS

Apocryphile Press
1100 County Route 54
Hannacroix, NY 12087
www.apocryphilepress.com

Please join our mailing list at www.apocryphilepress.com/free. We'll keep you up-to-date on all our new releases, and we'll also send you a FREE BOOK. Visit us today!

CONTENTS

INTRODUCTION

"Mystics in every faith report contacts with a world that startles
and transforms them with its dazzling darkness."
– Huston Smith[1]

The Cloud of Unknowing is one of the great classic texts of
Western mysticism. It is appropriate that the word "mysticism"
shares the same etymological root with the word "mystery"
since *The Cloud of Unknowing* argues that God ultimately
remains a mystery to us, always beyond the grasp of human
understanding. The etymological root that the words "mysticism" and "mystery" share is the ancient Greek word *muo*,
which means "to close one's eyes and one's mouth." It is where
we get the word "mute." So hidden within the word "mystic"
itself is an invitation to a key spiritual practice: the practice of
intentional silence, which is in fact the quintessential discipline
of mysticism. It is by quieting the mind, letting go of all the
chatter, and attending to the silence of our hearts that we open
ourselves up to a direct experience of God. This is how we
ourselves can become mystics, because mystics are simply

people who have had direct and unmediated experiences of the God who is beyond all knowing.

Jesuit theologian Karl Rahner said, "The Christian of the future will either be a mystic or will not exist at all."[2] He believed that if the Western church did not discover its mystical roots, then it would need to close its doors for good. Most people, it seems, are not thirsting for more doctrines and dogmas about God, but rather longing for a direct encounter with divine love. And this is exactly what the medieval author of *The Cloud of Unknowing* offers to its readers: a direct experience of the God who is beyond all dogmas and formulations. More specifically, he offers an ancient and practical method of meditation for encountering God not in our heads, but in our hearts.

Like all mystics, the *Cloud* author is deeply rooted in a particular faith tradition. Just as Jewish mystics like the Baal Shem Tov are rooted in Judaism and Sufi mystics like Rumi are rooted in Islam, so too is the author of *The Cloud of Unknowing* rooted in the Western Christian tradition. Mystics are members of faith communities that have peered under the stones of their tradition's doctrines and dogmas to discover the rich soil of direct spiritual experience. By delving deep into the radical roots of their own religion, mystics all seem to be tapping into a similar, if not identical, source. Although their faith traditions might appear to be drastically different on the surface, mystics all seem to be drinking from the same well. They may draw from different stories and use different symbols, but they all seem to be speaking a similar language to describe a shared experience.

By delving deep into the roots of his own tradition, the *Cloud* author ends up sounding almost like a Zen master or a teacher of Transcendental Meditation or the Taoist philosopher Lao Tzu, with poetic and enigmatic statements like "Be the wood, and let the [meditation] be the carpenter," "Pray nowhere," and "God is your Being."[3] In this way, mystical literature can offer a path for interreligious learning, dialogue, and growth, especially across the spiritual traditions of the East and West.

THE MEDIEVAL ENGLISH AUTHOR

The anonymous author of *The Cloud of Unknowing* is often referred to simply as the *Cloud* author because he is best known for writing this spiritual classic. Although he wrote and translated a handful of other spiritual texts (*The Book of Privy Counseling, A Letter on Prayer, The Assessment of Inward Stirrings, Hid Divinity*, and *Benjamin Minor*), it is *The Cloud of Unknowing* that towers above the rest in its originality, practicality, humor, creativity, and insight. The anonymity of the author seems to convey the hope that his readers remain undistracted by who he is. Similarly, his anonymity conveys the hope that we, as readers, remain undistracted by who *we* are, untethered by our egos and our false selves. The author invites us to get in touch with something much deeper: our Ground of Being, which is divine. He wants us to access the true self, not with our head, but with our heart.

The author was likely a Carthusian monk from a time and place characterized by turbulence, terror and spiritual creativity: 14th-century England. During this period, the Bubonic Plague, also known as the Black Death, was wiping out more than a third of England's population; the Hundred Years' War (between England and France) was well underway, claiming hundreds of young lives; and followers of the heretic and Bible translator John Wycliffe (known as the Lollards) were being burned at the stake all throughout England. Climate change, famine, and peasant protests and revolts convinced many that the world was nearing its apocalyptic end. And on top of all this, the people were quickly growing disillusioned with the Church and her leaders, who were proving just as power-hungry and abusive as the political leaders of the day, squabbling over rights of succession. It would have been easy for the *Cloud* author to be, like Martha of Bethany, deeply upset and overwhelmed about many things.

The fourteenth century was also a particularly fruitful and creative time spiritually in England. During this century, theologians in England started writing about God in their own vernacular language: in *English!* Most religious authors had previously written only in Latin. The *Cloud* author, who likely lived in the Beauvale Priory in Nottingham (the old stomping grounds of Robin Hood), was one of the first of these English theologians to write about God in the vernacular.

The *Cloud* author's English was Middle English, which is actually quite different than modern English. We could probably only pick out a handful of words and phrases here and there, and even those words and phrases likely meant something different back then compared to what they mean now. Nonetheless, it is still a version of English and English is an especially unique and versatile language. Because it is such a wonderfully complex and eclectic mix of Latin, German, Dutch, French, Celtic, Hebrew, Arabic, and more, the English language boasts more *synonyms* than any other language. In fact, some argue that the English language includes more total *words* than any other language.

When one has access to a new language, one can actually think novel thoughts and formulate fresh ideas because the brain has access to new words and concepts. Thus, medieval English theologians were able to think and articulate innovative and original ideas about the divine mystery. One of the most creative and innovative theologians of church history emerged in this era. She is known as Julian of Norwich and is the author of the first text written in English by a female. She boldly proclaimed that all perceptions of God as wrathful were human projections because ultimately "there is no wrath in God." She described God as a close friend, a lover, a king, a kind nurse, a courteous knight, as clothing, as a castle, as a cave, as a brother, as a father, and as the one true Mother. She wrote about experiencing God in the joy of laughter, in bodily pain and sickness, and even in the wondrous process of human digestion![4]

This rich theological tradition of seeing and experiencing God in the glorious beauty of our bodies and in the world around us is known as the cataphatic tradition. Cataphatic means "according to images" and refers to the many religious traditions that discover God's presence and reality in doctrines and ideas, in sanctuaries and sacraments, in icons and images, in bread and wine, and in hazelnuts and redwood trees. Julian was one of the greatest cataphatic theologians in church history, articulating her ideas in Middle English in a church anchorage in Norwich, about a hundred miles east of one of the greatest apophatic theologians.

THE APOPHATIC TRADITION

"In order to know everything, seek to know nothing."
—St. John of the Cross[5]

The anonymous author of *The Cloud of Unknowing* is not a part of the cataphatic tradition. Although he uses several images in his text, he remains part of another tradition: the apophatic tradition, which means "without images." The *Cloud* author and the apophatic tradition declare, "All those images and thoughts and ideas and doctrines about God are really good, but we all know that the infinite God can never be limited to *any* image, thought or idea." God is beyond all of that. All our ideas about God are just that: ideas *about God,* not God Himself. Thoughts about the divine are not the divine.

So the point of *The Cloud of Unknowing* is *not* to offer any new understanding of God. The point is rather to *let go* of all our understandings of God in order to experience God directly. This is why some refer to the apophatic tradition as "negative theology" or "dark contemplation." Of course, our direct experience of God might lead us to new insights and understandings about the divine, but the main point is not to gain new insights but to engage in a practice of letting go. Modern apophatic prayer practitioners such as William Meninger, Thomas Keating, and Basil Pennington call this practice of letting go "Centering Prayer" or "Contemplative Meditation."[6] The *Cloud* author refers to it simply as the "exercise" or the "work." Whatever you choose to call it, this practice involves relinquishing all our thoughts and ideas about God and opening ourselves up to an experience of God not with our knowledge, but with our love.

And who is this God whom we seek to love? The apophatic theologians answer, "God is Nothing." Or rather, "God is no thing." One of the most well-known apophatic theologians is the sixteenth-century Spanish mystic St. John of the Cross, who described God with three words: "Nada. Nada. Nada."[7] God is no thing because God is beyond all things. This does not mean that we reject our traditions' sacred texts, sacraments, and doctrines. Not at all. The *Cloud* author firmly believed that God speaks through the Scriptures, that the sacraments are sure and certain means by which we receive God's grace, and that God became incarnate in Jesus Christ. But the author also knew that God always exists beyond all of that. In Christ, all the fullness of God dwells;[8] however, our minds are finite and our vision limited. As the Apostle Paul says, "We see through a glass darkly."[9] We are all partially blind; so although the fullness of God may be embodied in Christ, our vision is not wide enough to completely comprehend the fullness of the ineffable and infinite God.

There is a story told in India about four blind men who were asked by a king to describe what an elephant looked like by feeling different parts of the elephant's body. One blind man felt the leg and said the elephant is like a pillar. Another felt the tail and said the elephant was like a rope. Another one felt the belly and said the elephant was like a wall, while the other felt the tusk and said the elephant was like a solid pipe. The king then said, "All of you are right. The reason every one of you is telling it differently is because each of you touched the different parts of the elephant. So actually, the elephant has all the features that you mentioned." Based on their own unique experiences they each arrived at their own different conclusions about the elephant. Instead of fighting over who had the correct conception of the elephant, they realized that they were all right. The *Cloud* author seems to have a similar understanding of God; his prayer practice offers a way to touch different parts of the "elephant" while still remaining faithful and true to one's own tradition.

To put it another way, the doctrines and ideas about God function as a finger pointing to the moon. Although we initially look at the finger to see which direction it is pointing, we need to stop looking at the finger once we see the moon. To obsess over the finger is not only inane – it is idolatry. The apophatic prayer practice taught in the *Cloud* helps us turn our attention away from the finger and towards the "moon" to which it points.

THE IMAGE TO LET GO OF IMAGES

> "Moses encountered the God who is
> beyond all knowledge and comprehension,
> for the text says, Moses approached
> the dark cloud where God dwelled."
> —Gregory of Nyssa[10]

"The source is called darkness."
—Tao Te Ching[11]

Even though the whole point of this meditation practice is to let go of all images, I am going to sketch out the prayer practice using images because that is exactly what the *Cloud* author does. The *Cloud* author essentially says, "OK, here's the image. Now let go of it." In other words, here's an image to help us let go of images, like the finger pointing to the moon.

The central image that the *Cloud* author uses is, of course, the cloud. Because the divine is beyond all human understanding, the author explains that God exists on the other side of what is called "the cloud of unknowing." This image is rooted in the biblical story of Moses, who heard the voice of God speak to him on Mount Sinai *from a cloud*.[12] Moses walked towards the cloud on Mount Sinai until he was enveloped by it. Early Christian theologians understood Moses to be the first apophatic mystic when he stepped into the darkness of that cloud to be with God.[13] St. Gregory of Nyssa called this cloud a "luminous darkness" and explained that Moses experienced a "seeing that consists in not seeing, because [the God whom he sought] transcends all knowledge, being surrounded on all sides by incomprehensibility as by a kind of darkness." This luminous darkness is the cloud of unknowing, which cannot be penetrated with thoughts. The anonymous author uses the image of an arrow (or a sword or a spear) to symbolize the only power that can pierce through the cloud to access God: that is, humble love. Then the author introduces another cloud called the "cloud of forgetting," under which he urges us to bury all of our thoughts, images and ideas. Along with the sword, we are also expected to carry a metaphorical shield, which we can use to deflect all our thoughts and send them back behind the cloud of forgetting.

Many years ago, I visited the magical island of Iona in the Scottish Hebrides, where the Irish pilgrim St. Columba arrived in the 6th century to found a monastery and give birth to Celtic Christianity in Scotland. During my visit, I hiked to the bay where St. Columba arrived about 1500 years ago, called St. Columba's Bay or the Bay of New Beginnings. According to tradition, pilgrims on the bay are invited to pick up two stones: the first stone, which represents new birth, is to be taken home; the second stone, which represents something that needs to be relinquished, is thrown into the ocean, into what the Celts call the "sea of forgetfulness." The *Cloud* author is using the same underlying principle: take one stone that symbolizes your love for God and hold it close to your heart. With that stone, you will be able to pierce the cloud of unknowing. Take another stone that represents all your thoughts, images, and ideas and hurl it behind the cloud of forgetting. Ultimately, even these thoughts and images of stones, clouds, swords, and shields are to be let go and forgotten as well.

THE PRAYER PRACTICE ITSELF

> "Can you step back from your own mind
> and thus understand all things?"
> —Tao Te Ching[14]

How exactly do we let go of these thoughts and images? The *Cloud* author recommends using a sacred word, preferably a monosyllabic word such as "God" or "Love." Some Christians become uncomfortable with this suggestion because of its resonance with Eastern meditation and mantras. However, this practice of using a sacred word in prayer stretches all the way back to the ancient roots of Christianity. John Cassian, Evagrius of Pontus, and the illustrious Desert Fathers and Mothers were repeating sacred words and phrases in their attempts to pray without ceasing back in the 4th and 5th centuries. According to the *Cloud* author, St. Mary of Bethany may have been using a sacred word in her prayer as she sat at the feet of Jesus.

This sacred word is to function as an anchor in the stream of consciousness. The word is a symbol of your love for God and thus the *sword* (or arrow or spear) that pierces through the cloud of unknowing. You are to return to this word whenever your mind starts to wander, and thus, the word is also that *shield,* deflecting all thoughts, images, and ideas that try to grab your attention. With this sacred word, you can simultaneously empty your mind and fill your heart. You can simultaneously hurl all thoughts behind the cloud of forgetting and shoot love through the cloud of unknowing. With this word, you can step back from your mind to establish a healthy detachment from your thoughts. In the words of Rumi, you can "move outside the tangle of fear-thinking" and "live in silence."[15]

Along with the words "God" and "Love," your sacred word might also be "Joy" or "Peace" or "Hope" or "Christ" or "Abba" or whatever else you feel best symbolizes your affection for God. The goal is to use that word to empty your mind and fill your heart with divine love, so don't think too much about the meaning of the word itself. Don't think about the word at all. In fact, don't think at all. Use the word to stop thinking. And start loving. That is the practice.

When it comes to specifics like breathing techniques, postures, and positions, this author doesn't seem to care. He actually warns his readers not to get too caught up in the details of form, technique, and location. He wants his readers to be "nowhere." So don't worry about how to sit or stand or kneel or levitate. The *Cloud* author doesn't care. All that matters is that you are loving God. That's it. Don't be worried and distracted by these other things. Only one thing is needed.

MARY AND MARTHA

One of the *Cloud* author's favorite passages of Scripture is from the Gospel of Luke, where Jesus is teaching at the home of Mary and Martha of Bethany. In this account, Martha becomes upset with Mary because, while she is busy preparing and serving food for the guests, Mary is peacefully sitting at the feet of Christ. Martha says to Jesus, "Lord, do you not care that my sister has left me to do all the work by myself? Tell her to help me." Jesus responds, "Martha, Martha, you are worried and distracted by too many things when only one thing is needed. And Mary has chosen it."[16]

The *Cloud* author upholds Mary of Bethany as the ideal practitioner and champion of the contemplative prayer practice that he is describing. He believes that as Mary sat at the feet of Jesus, she was piercing the cloud of unknowing. She was letting go of all thoughts, memories, and images, including the image of the human Jesus who was sitting right in front of her. She was also letting go of all the voices in her head, including the voice of her sister, who said, "You shouldn't just be sitting there. You should be busy helping me."

The author acknowledges the holiness of St. Martha and all her good works and the active life of service that she represents. However, whenever we engage in this sacred practice, we need to learn how to let go and lovingly ignore the voice of Martha, which is most often a voice within our own heads. If we try to sit still in the presence of God for 5, 10, or 15 minutes, we will most likely start to hear a voice saying, "Hey! You should really be doing something else right now. You have so much work to do. Stop this navel-gazing and do something useful." The *Cloud* author insists that this prayer practice is actually the most useful thing we can possibly do. So like Mary of Bethany, we need to learn to ignore all the noise and chatter inside our heads, including the criticism and complaints of our inner

Martha. There will always be things to be worried and upset about, but only one thing is needed: sitting in the presence of divine love.

THE INVITATION

This distillation of *The Cloud of Unknowing* is an invitation to enter into the mystical wisdom of the anonymous author from Nottingham, who responds to the question "Who is God?" with the humble words, "I don't know," but who then says, "That is not the right question to ask because it means you are still in your head. Get out of your head and into your heart." The English monk invites us into our hearts because he knows we cannot grasp God through knowledge, but we can embrace God through love. He invites us into our hearts, because in our hearts we already sense that God is the Love that holds the universe together, the Love that gives birth to the most distant stars, and the Love that breathes every breath of life with us and through us. So I invite you to meet God now in your heart.

OPENING COLLECT

Almighty God, to you all hearts are open,
all desires known, and from you no secrets are hid.
Cleanse the thoughts of our hearts
by the inspiration of your Holy Spirit
that we may perfectly love you
and worthily magnify your Holy Name,
through Christ our Lord. Amen.[1]

PROLOGUE: STOP

If you are reading this, I urge you to STOP.
By STOP, I literally mean "Stop reading"
for a moment and "take a breath."

Now "observe" what's going on inside you.
Specifically, I urge you to observe
and consider what you intuitively know
and believe about the divine.

Do you believe and have the
intuitive sense that God is Love?
Do you believe that God is the
self-giving Love that moves the sun
and other stars as well as the Love
that is closer to you than your very breath?

If not, please stop reading altogether.

If so, then "proceed."

1: DESIRE

The God who loves you with an everlasting love
has blessed you with the gift of existence
and has planted deep and holy desires
within your heart.

These deep desires and longings
have led you to this very moment.

The fact that you are reading these words
right now means that you are now ready
to dive headlong into the bottomless reservoir
of God's love and affection.

2: LET GO

One thing that will prove to be
a serious disservice to you in this process
is an overinflated ego. This is the part of you
that thinks you're better than everyone else
and in no need of God's mercy and grace.
This is the false self and it will always trip you up
and continually let you down.
Let it go. Now.

You are in the process of discovering your true self.
This process requires sober humility
and a healthy sense of self. Moreover,
it requires a humble and patient love for God.

3: THE CLOUD OF UNKNOWING

During the Holy Eucharist,
when the priest says,
"Lift up your hearts,"
the people respond,
"We lift them to the Lord."
That is exactly what I will be
teaching you how to do:
to lift up your heart to God.

In order to do this,
you need to practice letting go of *everything*
except your patient love for God.

As you let go and love God,
you will discover a darkness…

Do not be afraid.

This darkness is the cloud of unknowing.

It is the cloud that always exists
between you and God,
because God will always remain
beyond your knowing.

As you discover this darkness,
saints and angels will be throwing a party
in your honor.

4: LOVE

You will never be able to grasp God through knowledge.
So stop racking your brain!

"If you think you understand,"
said St. Augustine, "then it is not God."[1]

But listen to this miraculous secret:
Although God will never be
grasped through knowledge,
God can be embraced *through love.*

Whether you are a 24-year-old
or a 94-year-old (or a 4-month-old!),
you can embrace God through love.

In some ways,
this meditation practice is very easy.
In other ways, it will seem impossible.
It is like a river in which a child may wade
and an elephant can swim.[2]

It will require an enormous amount of patience.
So please take your time with this.

5: THE CLOUD OF FORGETTING

Let go of *everything*
except your patient love for God.

In order to penetrate
the cloud of unknowing through love,
you need to throw everything else
behind another cloud:
the cloud of forgetting.

And by "everything,"
I mean *everything*.
All your thoughts, images, and ideas.
Even the most holy and beautiful thoughts
you could ever think!
Do not even think about Christ or Mary
or saints and angels.

You're still in your head!
And God's not there.
God's waiting to meet you in your heart.

6: "I DON'T KNOW"

If you ask me,
"How can I best think about God?"
My answer is, "I don't know."

For God is to be loved, not understood.
The only way to pierce through
the thick cloud of unknowing
is with a sharp dart
of patient, humble love.

7: THE SINGLE WORD

During this practice, sweet thoughts
and brilliant insights will come
knocking on your door,
begging to be entertained.
This is not the time to invite them in.

They are to be sent back
behind the cloud of forgetting.

I strongly suggest you choose
and use a single word to help you with this.

I recommend the word "God"
or the word "Love."

This word will function as a kind of shield
to deflect all distractions.
With the strong shield of this single word,
all those distracting thoughts
and colorful insights

can be repelled and sent back
behind the cloud of forgetting.

This word will also function
as a kind of sword that can help
sharpen the focus of your love on God alone.
With this honed spear, your humble love
can pierce and penetrate
through the cloud of unknowing.

May this single word be spoken
in the silence of your heart,
in rhythm with your pulse.

In this way, the word will help you to be present
to the gratuitous gift of existence.

The word will help you to be rooted
in the Ground of Being.

The word will help you to be in tune
with the heartbeat of God.

8: DIFFERENT CALLINGS

You may be wondering about thoughts
that come to you which may increase
your compassion for Christ,
and which may bring you to tears
as you reflect on his Passion.

You may wonder,
"Aren't these good thoughts?"

I say, "Yes, indeed.
Receive them as God's sunbeams
shining down upon you."

At the same time,
be aware of how you *use* these thoughts.
They can easily swell your pride
and tighten your grip on the false self,
making you think, "Wow!
Aren't I a brilliant and insightful person!"

More importantly,
these generally good thoughts
can still distract you from the contemplative life:
the deeper work of loving God in the darkness.

Some people are primarily called to the active life,
which means striving for peace and justice
and caring for the weak, poor, and vulnerable.

Other people are primarily called
to the contemplative life.

Many are called to a combination of the two:
the "mixed life."

My friend, right now, I am inviting you
to consider a call to the contemplative life.
And in this life, only one thing is needed:
to sit peacefully before the God you love,
like Mary of Bethany.

Let go of all those distracting thoughts
and anxious voices that keep saying,
"You're not doing enough!"

Cover them up with a thick cloud of forgetting,
because only love can reach God.

9: USEFUL

You may think, "This is a waste of time.
I should be doing something more useful."
Believe me when I say:
this is *the most useful thing* you can possibly do.

You may think,
"This feels like self-centered navel gazing."
Believe me when I say
this is the *least* selfish thing you can do.
In fact, this is the most valuable
and beneficial thing you can do
for your friends and family,
including those who have died.

You may think,
"This would be much more useful and productive
if I could gain some profound insights
or receive some mystical experience…"

Although holy thoughts and insights

are very good in and of themselves,
they will remain distractions
to you in this practice.

Although mystical experiences
of divine warmth, sweetness, and song
may have some spiritual value,
they will often remain distractions
to you in the process of
piercing the cloud of unknowing.

So keep lifting your love up to that cloud.
Or rather, let God lift your love up to that cloud,
because there is nothing more useful or productive.

10-12: SINFUL THOUGHTS

Don't be surprised by the thoughts
that will come tumbling towards you
when you try to quiet your mind.

Not all of your thoughts will be holy.
In fact, many of them will probably be
disturbing or strange or downright evil.

If you try to fight these thoughts,
you will fail.
If you try to force yourself not to think them,
you will only be fanning the flame.
If you cut off your right hand
or gouge out your eye,
you won't accomplish anything,
because the thoughts will just keep coming back.

But thanks be to God!
Because these thoughts cannot hurt you.

Simply let the thoughts pass by,
like clouds in the sky, until they pass
behind that great cloud of forgetting.

And return again to your love for God,
which will uproot the ground of sin
and plant seeds of virtue within you.

13: HUMILITY

This practice will plant within you
the virtue of humility.

Humility is the awareness that,
without God's breath breathing within you,
you are but a corpse.

Likewise, if your heart and mind and soul
are disconnected from God's life and love,
then they remain empty shells,
which can easily grow moldy and rotten.

14: FALSE HUMILITY

You can experience true humility
by sensing your complete and utter dependence
upon God for every single breath you breathe.

You can also experience humility
by drinking a shot of God's love.

Humility that comes through
an experience of God's love
exceeds humility that comes through
an awareness of your emptiness.

However, once you think
you have attained humility,
you have already lost it.
As soon as you say, "I am humble,"
your soul will start releasing
the odor of foul-smelling pride.

15: PERFECT HUMILITY

Some say that perfect humility
can only be attained by acknowledging
how sinful and wretched we are.

I completely disagree.

I will admit that this might be effective
for some of us who sin frequently, like myself.

But if focusing on our sinful and wretched state
was the only way to attain perfect humility,
then our Lady St. Mary
and our Lord Jesus Christ
and all the angels in heaven
would not have perfect humility,
because they had no sinful state to contemplate.

Perfect humility can be experienced
through complete immersion

in God's love and grace.
So we can indeed be perfect by grace
just as God is perfect by nature.

16: MARY OF BETHANY

Mary of Bethany developed humility
not so much by focusing on her past sins,
but rather by sitting at the feet of Christ,
beaming her tender affection
upon the one who embodied God's Love.

We don't honor Mary of Bethany
because she wallowed in the stinking
swamp of her sins. No.

We honor Mary of Bethany
because her heart pulsated
with humble adoration for the one
who embodied God's Love.
In fact, I believe that when she was sitting
at the feet of Christ, she was actually
engaging in the very meditation
that I am inviting you to practice.
She was piercing through
the cloud of unknowing.

This is why Christ says,
"There is only one thing you need to do,
and Mary is doing it right now."[1]

17-21: ST. MARTHA'S COMPLAINTS

When we sit in the presence of God
like Mary of Bethany, we will often hear
the voice of Martha in our heads
complaining and urging us away
from this most important work.

Your inner Martha will want you to
stop "navel-gazing" and to help her
with all the busy work that needs to be done.

Please understand that much of Martha's work
is good and holy and necessary.
And thank God for Martha! She is truly a saint.

But also understand that
the work you're doing is *the most important* work
in the world for you right now.

So let Martha complain;
and let Jesus calm her anxieties.

Let go of any judgment
and let go of the need to defend yourself.
Jesus will defend you as he did Mary.

Just keep sitting silently in God's presence.

Let Martha's complaints pass by
like boats on a river, like clouds in the sky.

22: ANGELIC DISTRACTIONS

Mary of Bethany loved Jesus
with the same purity as Mary Magdalene.

When angels offered comfort to Mary Magdalene
at the tomb of Jesus and urged her
to discover him now risen in Galilee,
she refused to settle for such angelic comfort.

She remained at the tomb until
the Risen Christ appeared to her directly
because she knew that *when you seek*
an encounter with the king of angels,
an encounter with angels alone just won't do.

So in this practice,
keep piercing the cloud,
even if angels appear.

23: GOD'S DELIGHT

Some like to think that they're quoting
the Bible when they say,
"God helps those who help themselves."
My friend, you will not find this verse
in the sacred Scriptures.

Instead, in the sacred Scriptures, you will find this:
"Do not fret about food or clothing or shelter.
Your heavenly Father knows all your needs.
Simply beam with love in his holy presence
and he will take care of all the rest."[1]
God will give you an abundance of what you need.
If not, then God will give you
the spiritual and physical strength
to live your life fully
without these apparent necessities.
Either way, God's got you covered.

God delights in taking care of you.

So don't be distracted by the anxious concerns
and complaints of your inner Martha.
Don't worry about food or clothes or whatever.
Just keep piercing the cloud of unknowing
with your love.

In this way, you will have the opportunity
to taste perfect humility,
which comes from full immersion
in God's endless delight in you.

24: BEING WITH GOD

Sometimes we might feel driven to worship
and love God because of what we believe
we will get out of the relationship.
We think that if we love God,
we will be blessed with boundless pleasure and riches,
with health and wealth.

How would you feel if you learned
that a close friend loved you primarily
because you always bought him dinner
or gave him loads of cash?
Would that really be love?
And would that really be a close friend?

Isn't a close friend someone
who simply loves being around you?

This practice of piercing the cloud of unknowing
is really all about spending time with a close friend,

not for the sake of free dinner or extra cash,
but simply because you love being around him.

25: HOLY AFFECTION

By simply spending time with God in this way,
you will naturally start cultivating the virtues
of equanimity and impartiality towards others.

With these virtues, you will be able
to extend love and generosity to all people,
even to people you might not particularly like.

Although you will still have a special affection
for your close friends
(just as Jesus had for his friends
John, Mary Magdalene, and Peter),
you will develop, through this practice,
a holy affection for the entire human family.

26: BOTH EASY AND HARD

I said that this meditation practice is quite easy.
It is indeed.

And it is also very, very hard.

The hard part is letting go of all of your
thoughts, images, and memories
and dropping them all underneath
the cloud of forgetting.

The easy part is simply sitting
in the presence of the God who loves you.
Yes, the easy part is simply spending quality time
with the God who is always waiting to be with you.

When you rest in God's presence,
you may occasionally experience
God piercing through the cloud of unknowing
in love towards *you*.
Rather than the other way around.

If and when this happens,
be prepared for your heart
to be set aflame
by the wildfire
of God's love.

(I won't be like those annoying babblers
and say much more about this fire of love,
because such divine secrets cannot be uttered
by any human tongue.)[1]

27-29: DIVINE THERAPY

Why is it so profoundly difficult
to simply sit still in silence?
Because whenever we are silent
for more than a few minutes,
all of our shadows and secrets and sins
come to the surface of our consciousness.

Jesus says, "Whenever you pray,
go into your closet and close the door."[1]

Surely, Jesus knows about all the
skeletons we like to hide in our closets.

And Jesus wants prayer to be the place
where we confront these skeletons
and face our fears.

If we do not confront the skeletons in our closets, then they will
control the whole house.
If we do not expose our shadows,

then they will run the whole show.

This is why some say
that all of humanity's problems
stem from our inability to sit quietly
in a room alone.[2]

Because when we fail to confront our shadows,
then our unconsciousness starts pulling the strings
and we become mere puppets
shoved around by selfishness and greed.

But by confronting the skeletons in our closet
in the context of prayer,
we allow divine therapy to commence.[3]
And then the dark closet of our secret sins
can become a holy sanctuary
where God's resplendent light
can gleam and grow.

30: EXPOSE THE SHADOW

If you notice that secret sins and shadows
just won't stop harassing you
during this meditation, then stop.
Go and confess your sins to a priest.

After you have exposed the shadow in confession,
it will lose much of its power.
In fact, it will no longer be a shadow,
because it has now been exposed to the light.

If you are not harassed by secret sins and shadows,
do not take this as an opportunity
to judge others and to feel better about yourself
at other people's expense.

Judge yourself if you like,
but leave others alone.

31-32: SOME TRICKS IF SHADOWS
PERSIST

If troubling thoughts and past sins
keep harassing you even after
you have confessed them, then boldly
tread them under your feet and
cover them with the cloud of forgetting.

And if this doesn't work,
I suggest the following two techniques...

First, ignore them as if you were
looking over their shoulders
to lock eyes with someone else behind them.
(That "someone else" is God,
who is surrounded on all sides
by the cloud of unknowing.)
Don't give those troubling thoughts and past sins
the satisfaction of your frustration.
The more you try to fight them,
the stronger they will become.
But if you are indifferent to them,

then they will eventually leave you alone.

Second, if you cannot let go
of these troubling thoughts,
then simply say to God, "I give up.
I cannot stop thinking these thoughts,
even though I have tried.
So I lay this whole situation in your hands
and relinquish myself of all responsibility
for the thoughts that I can no longer control
on my own. God, you are now fully responsible."
After praying this prayer,
the troubling thoughts may very likely
continue to persist, but you need not worry at all.
It is no longer your problem.
It is God's problem now.
So let the troubling thoughts persist
as much as they like while you gently melt
into the ocean of God's endless love for you.

33: TEACHING REST

Once you have tested out these techniques for yourself,
you will be able to teach them better than me.

By engaging in this practice,
you will be able to teach others
how to find deep rest in the midst of stress
and holy silence in the midst of anxious chatter.

Although we cannot fully enjoy the great heavenly rest
while we remain in our human bodies,
this prayer practice offers us a taste
of that perfect grace.

34: CONSENT

Let the perfect grace have its way with you.
When it asks for your consent, say, "Yes."
Be the wood, and let it be the carpenter.
Be blind and let go of your desire to know.

If you don't understand what I'm saying,
that's OK. Much of this will make sense to you
after you have had your own direct experience
of God's love.

Don't let any priest get in the way.

35: THE MIRROR OF PRAYER

Sometimes when you sit down to pray in this special way,
you will feel tired and restless.
Pray anyway.

And please understand that "prayer" can include much more
than this particular practice of piercing the cloud.

Prayer can also include reading books of spiritual value,
reflecting on sacred Scripture,
listening to inspiring sermons,
gathering with the saints in song,
sauntering through the forest with a grateful heart,
and drinking from the well of the church's ancient wisdom.

Just as you use a glass mirror to see your face,
use these forms of prayer to peer into your soul.

And with these mirrors,
you can wipe the spiritual schmutz off your face.

36: SOUL AND BODY

When you pray by penetrating the cloud of unknowing,
you will come to see your soul as utterly dependent
on God's goodness and benison.

And you will come to know that,
apart from God's breath breathing in and through you,
your body is nothing more than a corpse,
a lumpy wad of flesh.

37: PERKING UP THE EARS OF HEAVEN

This prayer practice will stir within you
a deep love and appreciation for the
Church's already potent prayers and ancient Collects.

You will also learn to appreciate
the power of brevity in prayer.

Just one short word perks up the ears of the heavens
more than a thousand empty phrases.

According to the wisdom of Ben Sira,
"The short prayer of a humble person
shoots past the clouds and keeps on going
until it reaches the Lord Most High,
who will respond with swift justice."[1]

38: GOD'S FULLNESS

If you hear someone yell "Fire!" or "Help!"
you will pay attention, right?
Even if it's an annoying neighbor,
you will still get out of your comfortable bed
in order to see what's going on and try to help.

Similarly, by praying with your one short word,
you will get God's attention—and God's help.

Or to put it another way, you will come to notice
the loving attention that God is already giving you,
every day, and in every moment.

You will come to notice God filling you with his fullness,
with the wideness of his mercy,
with the breadth of his love,
with the height of his glory,
and with the depth of his wisdom.

39-40: INHALE "GOD," EXHALE "SIN"

There are two short words that seem to sum up everything:
"God" and "sin."

I invite you to breathe in all of God's goodness
as you say the word "God,"

and to release all the sickness of sin
as you say the word "sin."

Breathe in "God."
Breathe out "Sin."

God in.
Sin out.

41-42: MODERATION

Please take good care of your body
for it is a temple of the Holy Spirit.

Get plenty of exercise and lots of sleep.
Read good books and have stimulating conversations.
Eat and drink, but not too much.

Practice moderation in all things, except this.

There is no need for moderation
when it comes to piercing the cloud of unknowing.
There is no need for moderation when it comes to
breathing in "God" and breathing out "sin."

Give yourself over to this practice with reckless abandon.
Be of good health so that you can pray this prayer
more often and for longer periods of time.

Breathe God in.
And breathe sin out.

When you are in good health, pray.
And when you are in poor health, pray.

God in.
Sin out.

God in.
Sin out.

God
in.

Sin
out.

43: LUMP

You have no being apart from God.

You are simply a lump of clay through which God breathes his
exquisite being.

To believe that you can exist apart from God
is to put your faith in a fetid lump of flesh.
So let go of that belief.
Throw it behind the cloud of forgetting.

Remember:
God in.
Sin out.

44: EXISTENCE AS GIFT

Relinquish the part of you that believes
you have earned your existence
by virtue of your own personal greatness.

Let go of the self who thinks that it holds value
apart from its connection to God.

Always remember that your existence is a gift,
a gratuitous gift from the God
who breathes you into being.

Embrace the part of you that finds
self-worth and value in divine love and grace.

Cherish the part of you that believes
you have received your being as a birthday present
from the One who made you.
By receiving this present, you can learn
to accept yourself as nobility, as royalty,
as holy and most worthy of love.

45: BEWARE OF WARM FUZZIES

You are most worthy of love and most worthy *to love*.
So lift up your heart to God,
but don't be stupid about it.

Don't expect your love for God
to feel like a schoolgirl crush.
Don't expect warm fuzzies
and butterflies in your stomach.
Don't expect to feel an inner passion
which some people call the "fire of love."

Such expectations and feelings
will prove to be distractions,
and sometimes very dangerous distractions.

46: PLAY

For the love of God, do not treat the Divine
like a helpless prey that you can catch and devour
with your effort and brute strength.

Prayer is not a weapon to help
monsters and predators wolf up victims.

Remember the consequence for the greedy beasts who
approached the cloud of unknowing
on Mount Sinai? They were pummeled with stones![1]

Avoid such a pummeling.

Be patient with God
and be with patient with yourself.

God is looking for ways to play with you,
like a father plays with his beloved child.

Let God kiss you and embrace you

and play hide-and-seek with you.

Although this may sound childish and foolish,
you will soon discover the truth of God's playful grace.

You will learn that God is no helpless prey,
but rather the most glorious power in the universe
who deigns to be your daddy, eager to play.

To sum up (in a playful way):
pray not for prey,
but for play.

47: YOUR SECRET HIDING PLACE

This talk of hide-and-seek with God
is not to be dismissed as silly childishness.
The God who is hidden beyond the cloud of unknowing
longs to find you at prayer
in your secret hiding place.

As Jesus taught, "When you pray,
do not babble like the religious hypocrites
in their temples of self-righteousness.
Rather, go to your secret hiding place,
close the door, and pray to the God
who is beyond all knowing. Your God,
who sees what is done in secret, will reward you."[1]

When you pray in your secret hiding place,
you better buckle up, because the Almighty God,
to whom all hearts are open, all desires known,
and from whom no secrets are hid,
will find you there. And when he does,

he will tumble over you with his love
and grant you the secret desires of your heart.

48: THE WINDOW OF YOUR SENSES

If your love for God compels you to pray aloud
the gentle name of Jesus,
then go ahead and do it.

If your prayer practice wipes the window
of your senses clean so that you receive
the sweet tastes and sounds of heaven,
then let them come. Even welcome them.

But do not get carried away
by these feelings and sensations.
The tastes and sounds and aromas
that come in through the window of your senses
can be very dangerous distractions.

Another man has written about this subject
and his eloquence is a hundred times
more refined than mine.[1] So let's move on.

49: ALL YOU NEED IS HUMBLE LOVE

All you need is humble love.
Everything else is negligible.

This humble love for God will be your guide
in this life and it will lead you to the rich banquet
prepared for you in the life to follow.

So let God stir up this humble love within you.

Let it be activated by every good gift that God gives you,
which is everything.

50: MORE HUMBLE, LESS GRUMBLE

Whether or not you experience
warm fuzzies or holy tears,
deep insights or poor health,
let humble love shape and form
your prayer and your will.

Because the more your love is humble,
the less your heart will gripe and grumble.

51: IS GOD "WITHIN"?

God indeed dwells within us.

However, this does not mean that we need
to roll our eyes in towards the back of our heads
in order to try catching a peek
of the God who is within.

Do not take the word "within" literally.
Do not try turning your bodily senses inward
in order to catch a glimpse of your brain and heart.

If you try to do this, you can easily
fall into a different kind of meditation,
a kind of "navel-gazing" that easily leads
to selfishness, narcissism, and sin.

52-53: SHOWING OFF

Be wary of experiencing heavenly light,
sweet aromas,
luscious tastes in your mouth, and
burning pleasures in your breasts and loins.

Although these may feel enjoyable,
they are likely fabricated and are often
telltale signs that you are trying to show off.

Signs that you are trying to show off
include, but are not limited to:
Staring wildly like a madman,
mistaking your mouth for your ear
and gaping it open in order to listen,
moving your arms as if swimming through the air,
tilting your head as if a worm were in your ear,
twiddling your thumbs,
tapping your feet,
waggling,

gurgling,
juggling,
spluttering,
squeaking.

(And speaking of squeaking…)

54: AVOID THE POMPOUS PIPSQUEAK

When you engage regularly in this practice,
don't be surprised
if people start becoming attracted to you.
By drenching yourself in divine grace,
you will become a source of grace for others.

People will experience you as
awash with wisdom, full of holy fire,
and abundant with spiritual fruit.

But if you pursue this practice
merely for the sake of these benefits,
then you will be sipping the poison of spiritual pride
and will quickly become an annoying pipsqueak
with an overinflated ego.

55-56: THE SOFT WAY TO HELL (OR, THE DEVIL'S NOSTRIL)

In Hebrew, the word for the devil is the "Satan," which means the "Accuser."

Whenever we get caught up
in the compulsion to falsely *accuse* others
and to blame them for our own mistakes,
then we are succumbing
to the sick behavior of the Satan.

When we derive pleasure
from other people's failures and faults,
then we will start to reek like the devil,
who (so I have heard)
has only one
nostril.

What does this mean?

Let me explain.
The septum of the nose is a symbol

of our ability to discern between good and evil,
truth and falsehood.

The devil, who has no septum,
seeks to convince us that
all of our convoluted conspiracies are true,
especially those conspiracies
in which we are perfectly innocent
and everyone else is horribly guilty.

Some of my necromancer friends
have told me that when the devil appears,
he likes to lift up his nostril to reveal his brain,
which is nothing more than the fires of hell.
When you look, you lose your mind.

Whether or not this is true,
we know the devil wants us to lose our ability
to discern between truth and falsehood.
The devil wants us to lose our minds.

The devil's conspiracies may sound convincing
and even consoling at first,
but they are ultimately heresies
that merely provide more cushioning
on the soft way to hell.

57-60: GOD IS NOT "UP" THERE

God is not a bearded old white man
sitting on a throne *up* in heaven.

"But," you might ask,
"didn't St. Martin of Tours look *up*
and see God wearing his royal robe in heaven,
surrounded by angels?

"And didn't St. Stephen look *up*
and see Christ standing next to God's throne?"[1]

And didn't Christ himself ascend *up*
into the heavens to sit at God's right hand?"[2]

Yes indeed, but do not take the word "up" literally.
These stories are not intended to convey
a physical reality, but a spiritual truth.

These stories are like the rough shell
surrounding the sweet kernel inside.

They are like the beautiful chalice
from which we drink the wine.

As one might kiss a cup
because of the superb cordial inside,
so too do we honor these stories
because of the truth they contain.

We are not like those reckless ingrates
who, after drinking from a beautiful cup,
smash it against the wall.

And what is the truth contained
in these stories about God being "up" there?

Well, there are many spiritual truths
contained in these stories,
but the one I want to share with you
is perhaps the most ironic and counterintuitive:

Whenever God reveals Godself as "up" there,
we are invited to see God as down here,
right beside us, especially in the midst of our suffering.

It was by standing up in heaven
that Christ was saying to St. Stephen,
"I stand by you; and I stand by all who suffer."

And it was by ascending that Christ
poured down the Holy Spirit,
who is also called the Paraclete,
which means the "One who stands beside us."
Ultimately, of course, God is nowhere.

And yet God is now here,
in the sacrament of the present moment.
Seek God and receive God there with gratitude.[3]

Remember: the road to heaven
is measured not in miles,
but desires.

61-66: DESIRE THE TRUE SELF

As Jesus ascended bodily into heaven,
this prayer practice will help you
ascend spiritually into your true self.

When you consider the unblushing benefits
of discovering your true self,
you will likely find that your desires
are not too strong, but rather too weak.

Your true self breathes in tune
with the divine breath.

Your true self is powered by
a mind with miraculous potential,
a purpose enlightened by reason,
and a will at rest in God.

Your true self is powered by
an imagination that is mastered by grace
and a sensuality that delights in all of God's thrilling gifts.

The false self, on the other hand,
remains far too easily satisfied in the mud,
wallowing around like swine. [1]

67: THE TRUE SELF IS ONE WITH GOD

My friend, please do not misunderstand me
when I say your true self is one with God.

God is your being, but you are not God.[1]
The greatest danger is to confuse
your ego and your false self with God.

When you engage in this prayer practice,
you become one with God *by grace.*

Listen to me:
You become divine by grace.

Remember when Jesus quoted
Psalm 81 in the Gospel of John?
He said, "You are Gods."[2]

He was teaching us that, by grace,
we can become what God is by nature.

68: NOTHING AND NOWHERE

Don't try to attain this oneness with God
by going within yourself.

"Then where should I go?" you ask.

I tell you, "Go nowhere."

"Do nothing."

Earnestly do nothing.
Persist in doing nothing
as long as you do it for God's love.

This nothing and nowhere is infinitely greater
than everything and everywhere.

This nothing and nowhere is not seen, but felt.

It is an obscure darkness because
it is an overabundance of spiritual light.

To the naked eye, it is nothing.

To the spiritual eye, it is All.

69: DON'T GIVE UP

In the midst of this nothing and nowhere,
you may become painfully aware
of your mortality and finitude.
You may feel like a lump of sin,
a bag of dirt,
and even a lifeless corpse,
but don't give up.

After wading through this hell-like purgatory,
the joyful consolation of God's breath
will come rushing through you
and you two will become one.

But don't forget:
as long as you have a body,
the cloud of unknowing will remain
between you and God.

70: ST. DENYS AND THE SENSES (AND CITATIONS)

Persist diligently in this nothing and nowhere
and don't get distracted by the bodily senses.
They won't help you with this practice.

With your eyes, you can only see
shapes, sizes, depths and colors.
With your ears, you can only hear noises.
With your nose, you can only smell stenches.
With your mouth, you can only taste that which is
sweet, sour, salty, fresh, bitter, or pleasant.
With your skin, you can only touch that which is
hot, cold, hard, tender, soft or sharp.

But with this prayer practice,
you will develop your spiritual senses.

And with your spiritual senses,
you will learn to explore the inexhaustible expanse
of God's playground.

However, no matter how enhanced
your spiritual powers may become,
you will still not fully comprehend
the God who is beyond all knowing.

As St. Denys says,
"The truly divine knowledge of God
is that which is known by unknowing."[1]

(Some might suggest that I add
a citation to this quote, but I won't.

Everything I have said so far
—and everything that I will say—
can be corroborated by the works of St. Denys.

People used to think it was a sign of humility
to be constantly citing Scripture
and the sayings of the church fathers.

But now this custom has devolved into
an arrogant display of academic grandstanding.

You don't need that,
so I'm not going to do it.)

70-72: MOSES, AARON, AND THE ARK

For some, this prayer practice
may come quite naturally
and the grace of contemplation
may linger with them
throughout their everyday lives.

For others, it will take a great deal of time and work.

I invite you to think of the grace of contemplation
as the Ark of the Covenant.

Aaron the High Priest represents
the person for whom this prayer practice
comes easily and who receives
the grace of contemplation right away.
As the priest of the Temple,
he was able to touch and see
the Ark of the Covenant whenever he pleased.

Moses, on the other hand,

represents the person for whom this prayer practice
takes much time and labor.
It was only after climbing the mountain
and spending six days in
the great cloud of unknowing
that God showed Moses a glimpse
of the Ark and provided him
with instructions on how to build it.
And even after all that time and work,
Moses still did not see the Ark
with the same frequency as Aaron.

Moses and Aaron represent two poles
on a long spectrum of spiritual experiences.

So withhold your judgement
and don't expect others to have
the same experience as you
when it comes to this prayer practice.

73: I AM BEZALEL

There was another man who was
intimately involved with the Ark of the Covenant
and whose experience should be added
to the spiritual spectrum.
I am talking about the man named
Bezalel who built the Ark.[1]

Moses, who worked hard,
was given a glimpse of the Ark.
Aaron, who maintained the Ark,
could see and touch it whenever he pleased.

Bezalel, who built the Ark, could only see it
after he made it and fashioned it
according to the instructions
Moses received from the mountain.

My spiritual friend, although I am not worthy
to be called a teacher,
when it comes to this prayer practice,

I hold the office of Bezalel.

For your sake, I am trying to make plain for you
the grace of contemplation as I have received it.

I am trying to build and fashion for you
the spiritual ark.

And if I am Bezalel, then may you be Aaron.

May this prayer practice come to you easily and naturally.

May you receive the grace of contemplation
the way Aaron received the Ark;
and may your spiritual gifts
outweigh my ineptitude.

74: TAKE IT OR LEAVE IT

If this prayer practice does not suit your disposition,
then simply leave it and pursue another spiritual discipline.
I will not be offended.

My humble purpose has been to help you
progress deeper into the heart of God,
in the best way I know how.

So I invite you to take it or leave it,
but if you take it, please honor the following conditions:

If this prayer practice resonates with you,
then I urge you to read these words of mine again.
Reread them every year or so.
The more often the better,
because the more often you read,
the more you will understand.
In fact, you will soon understand more than me.

Do not share this book with those
whom you already know will not be disposed to it.

If you do share it with others, please urge them
to read all my words, not just a line here or there.

Finally, keep this book away from
the chatterboxes and the rumormongers,
the gossips and the pipsqueaks,
the tittle-tattlers and the faultfinders,
the holy rollers and the Bible thumpers,
the pious grandstanders and the spiritual show-offs,
and also the superficial religious folk.

This book is not for them.

75: HOLY DESIRES

Some will read this book
and resonate with its content.
Although this may be the result of intellectual curiosity,
it may also be evidence of a deeper calling.

If you want to learn whether or not
you are called to this prayer practice,
then discuss it with your priest
and your spiritual director.
If both your priest and spiritual director
encourage you to explore the calling,
then go for it.

Signs that you are called to pursue this practice
include, but are not limited to:

Finding that all other spiritual disciplines
pale in comparison to this prayer practice.

Experiencing this prayer as your secret little love.

Feeling hounded every day
by the desire to pray in this way.

Understanding any lack of desire for it
as God's invitation for you to let go of pride.

Growing in your sense that God
is always your friend and never your enemy.

Understanding that whenever grace is withdrawn,
God is expanding your heart,
preparing your soul, and deepening your desire
for the great banquet he has prepared for you.

Tasting one sip of God's wine
and enjoying an ecstasy
that outweighs the sorrow you felt in longing for it.

As St. Gregory the Great said,
"All holy desires grow by delay;
and if they diminish by delay
then they were never holy desires."[1]

And St. Augustine summed it all up when he said,
"The whole of life for a Christian
is nothing else but holy desires."[2]

When God looks at you with his merciful eyes,
it is not what you are
or what you have been
that he sees
but who you desire to be.

81

So, my friend, may your holy desires grow.

And may you find true peace, sane wisdom,
and spiritual comfort in knowing that
whenever God looks at you,
he takes great delight in you
and is immensely proud to call you his own.

And the blessing of God,
the Father, the Son, and the Holy Spirit
be with you and remain with you
and all of God's lovers here on earth,
now and forever.

Amen.

NOTES

INTRODUCTION

1. Huston Smith, *The World's Religions: Our Great Wisdom Traditions* (San Francisco: HarperOne, 2009), 130.
2. Karl Rahner, *Theological Investigations VII*, trans. David Bourke (New York: Herder and Herder, 1971), 15.
3. *The Cloud of Unknowing*, Chs. 34, 68, 67; *The Book of Privy Counseling*, Ch 1.
4. Julian of Norwhich, *Showings*, trans. Edmund Colledge and James Walsh (Mahwah NJ: Paulist Press, 1978).
5. St. John of the Cross, *Ascent of Mount Carmel*, 13. 11.
6. See William Meninger, *The Loving Search for God: Contemplative Prayer and the Cloud of Unknowing* (New York: Continuum, 1998); Thomas Keating, *Open Mind, Open Heart* (New York: Bloomsbury Continuum, 2019); Basil Pennington, *Centering Prayer: Renewing an Ancient Christian Prayer Form* (New York: Image, 1982).
7. St. John of the Cross, *Ascent of Mount Carmel*.
8. Colossians 2:9.
9. 1 Corinthians 13:12.
10. St. Gregory of Nyssa, *The Life of Moses*, Book II. 164.
11. Lao Tzu, *Tao Te Ching: A New English Version*, Ch. 1, trans. Stephen Mitchell (New York: Harper Perennial, 1988).
12. Exodus 24:16.
13. Exodus 20:21.
14. Lao Tzu, *Tao Te Ching*, Ch. 10.
15. Rumi, *The Essential Rumi*, trans. Coleman Barks with John Moyne (New York: Harper Collins, 1995), 3.
16. Luke 10:38-42.

OPENING COLLECT

1. Some trace this prayer back to St. Alcuin of York (735 – 804) who may have written it for the consecration of Charlemagne, warning the great king of the divine King from whom no secrets are hid, including any clandestine political motivations lurking behind the religious ceremony. The prayer can be found in Latin in the Leofric missal, an illuminated manuscript from the 10th and 11th century, named after Leofric, the Bishop of Exeter. It is also listed in the Sarum Rite (again in Latin) among the prayers said privately by the priest before Mass. Established by St. Osmond the Bishop

of Salisbury (d. 1099), the Sarum Rite served as an adapted Roman Rite to be used in the Salisbury Cathedral and throughout the Salisbury Diocese. The Sarum Rite or Use of Salisbury spread in popularity throughout England, likely inspiring the anonymous author of *The Cloud of Unknowing* to translate it into his Middle English. The Archbishop of Canterbury Thomas Cranmer (d. 1556) dipped into the Sarum Rite as a resource in constructing his 1549 Book of Common Prayer and plucked this jewel of a prayer. Influenced by Reformation theology and the belief in the priesthood of all believers, Cranmer decided to make the prayer into a communal one to be prayed by all who are gathered for worship, not just the priest. Today, the prayer, known as the Collect for Purity, is prayed towards the beginning of the Holy Eucharist service in nearly all Anglican rites throughout the global Anglican Communion. Episcopalians pray the prayer as written in the 1979 Book of Common Prayer on page 323 of Holy Eucharist Rite I and on page 355 of Holy Eucharist Rite II, which is how I have rendered it here, *undistilled.*

4: LOVE

1. St. Augustine, *Sermon 117,* Patrologia Latina (PL) 38. Although the *Cloud* author does not cite St. Augustine in this chapter, the fact that he cites him in the last chapter (Ch. 75) inspired me to use this pithy quote to distill the author's argument.
2. This is a reference to a quote attributed to St. Gregory the Great, who said, "Scripture is like a river...shallow enough for the lamb to wade, but deep enough for the elephant to swim." *Letter to Leander* 4, *Moralia,* Corpus Christianorum Series Latina (CCSL) 143:6.

16: MARY OF BETHANY

1. Luke 10:42.

23: GOD'S DELIGHT

1. See Matthew 6:25-34.

26: BOTH EASY AND HARD

1. This is likely a derogatory reference to the 14th-century English hermit and mystic Richard Rolle, who wrote a book about his mystical experiences titled *Incendium Amoris,* which translates from the Latin into English as "The Fire of Love."

27-29: DIVINE THERAPY

1. Matthew 6:6.
2. This is my reference to a quote by Blaise Pascal (1623 – 1662), who said, "Tout le malheur des hommes vient d'une seule chose, qui est de ne savoir pas demeurer en repos dans une chambre." *Pensées* 139. Obviously, the *Cloud* author did not reference Pascal, but I use it to demonstrate the universality of this wisdom.
3. See Thomas Keating, *On Divine Therapy* (Brooklyn NY: Lantern Books, 2012).

37: PERKING UP THE EARS OF HEAVEN

1. Ecclesiasticus 35:17. This verse from Ecclesiasticus (or the Book of Sirach or simply Ben Sira) is not included in the original *Cloud* text but is included in Walsh's translation, in a note that highlights the rich history of early Christian teaching on the power of short prayers. This verse seems especially appropriate as it references how short prayers can pierce through the "cloud." *The Cloud of Unknowing,* trans. James Walsh (Mahwah NJ: Paulist Press, 1981), 193, n. 264.

46: PLAY

1. See Exodus 19:12-24 and Hebrews 12:18-21.

47: YOUR SECRET HIDING PLACE

1. Matthew 6:5-7.

48: THE WINDOW OF YOUR SENSES

1. The author is likely referring to the 14th-century English Augustinian mystic and theologian Walter Hilton (1340 – 1396), who writes about bodily sensations during mystical experience in Chapter 11 of Book One of *The Ladder of Perfection.*

57-60: GOD IS NOT "UP" THERE

1. Acts 7:57.
2. Mark 16:19.
3. Here I am riffing on the following quote from Evelyn Underhill: "God is always coming to you in the Sacrament of the Present Moment. Meet and receive Him there with gratitude in that sacrament." Evelyn Underhill, *Life as Prayer and Other Writings of Evelyn Underhill*, ed. Lucy Menzies (Harrisburg PA: Morehouse, 1991), 185 – 186.

61-66: DESIRE THE TRUE SELF

1. The *Cloud* author's reference to "swine wallowing in the mud" inspired this riff on C. S. Lewis's famous lines: "If we consider the unblushing promises of reward and the staggering nature of the rewards promised in the Gospels, it would seem that Our Lord finds our desires not too strong, but too weak. We are half-hearted creatures, fooling about with drink and sex and ambition when infinite joy is offered us, like an ignorant child who wants to go on making mud pies in a slum because he cannot imagine what is meant by the offer of a holiday at the sea. We are far too easily pleased." C. S. Lewis, *The Weight of Glory and Other Addresses* (New York: Harper Collins, 2001), 26.

67: THE TRUE SELF IS ONE WITH GOD

1. In Chapter 1 of *The Book of Privy Counseling*, the *Cloud* author writes, "He is your being and in him, you are what you are, not only because he is the cause and being of all that exists, but because he is *your* cause and the deep center of *your* being." *The Cloud of Unknowing*, trans. Phyllis Hodgson (New York: Image, 1973), 150.
2. John 10:34.

70: ST. DENYS AND THE SENSES (AND CITATIONS)

1. Pseudo-Dionysius, "The Divine Names" Ch. 7, 872B in *Pseudo-Dionysius: The Complete Works*, trans. Colm Luibheid (Mahwah NJ: Paulist Press, 1987), 109. Although the *Cloud* author frowned upon citations, St. Denys deserves his due: in the fifth century CE, a Syrian monk used the name of the biblical character Dionysius the Areopagite (Acts 17:34) as a pseudonym in writing books about the God beyond all knowing. The author likely chose this name because he imagined Dionysius had been deeply persuaded

by St. Paul's teaching about the "unknown God" (Acts 17:23), a phrase that inspired the author to formulate the foundations of apophatic theology. The *Cloud* author assumed that this author was indeed the biblical character who later became the first bishop of Athens, according to church historian Eusebius (*Ecclesiastical History* Book III.iv) and so referred to him as St. Denys. Today, this Syrian author is referred to as Pseudo-Dionysius or Pseudo-Denys.

73: I AM BEZALEL

1. Exodus 36:1 – 38: 31.

75: HOLY DESIRES

1. St. Gregory the Great, *Homilia in Evangelia* II, 25, Patrologia Latina (PL) 76, 1190 as cited in *The Cloud of Unknowing,* trans. Walsh, 265.
2. St. Augustine, *In Epistolam Joannis ad Parthos,* IV, 6, as cited in *The Cloud of Unknowing,* trans. Walsh, 266.

Made in United States
North Haven, CT
28 April 2022

18689516R00067